CW00393831

The Message of Carmel at Aylesford

by
Francis Kemsley O.Carm.

All booklets are published thanks to the
generous support of the members of the
Catholic Truth Society

CATHOLIC TRUTH SOCIETY
PUBLISHERS TO THE HOLY SEE

Contents

Carmel in England

In the English county of Kent, a mile from the Pilgrims' Way which leads from London to Canterbury, lies the pretty village of Aylesford. The medieval Carmelite Priory there, commonly known as The Friars, is today a major pilgrimage destination. Alongside a number of well-preserved medieval buildings the modern Shrine to the Blessed Virgin Mary - Our Lady of the Assumption - provides a welcome and facilities for the many pilgrims (Catholic and others) who come from far and wide. Aylesford is not only the largest Roman Catholic shrine in Southwark Archdiocese but one of the most popular pilgrimage destinations in Britain, attracting some quarter of a million visitors a year. Some come simply for a nice day out in pleasant surroundings. Others come looking for something deeper; the message of Carmel. All are welcome.

Centuries ago the Carmelite friars at Aylesford offered hospitality to pilgrims travelling to the shrine of St Thomas Becket at Canterbury. During the Protestant Reformation the friars were expelled from their home, but since their return in 1949 the Priory has become a place of pilgrimage in its own right.

The concept of pilgrimage is important in all our world's religions. We leave our homes and all that is familiar to travel to a holy place. Penance and thanksgiving may be part of our journey. Arriving at the shrine a pilgrim encounters God in a particular way, being spiritually transformed and strengthened, before returning home with new vigour. During the Middle Ages Canterbury and Walsingham were the principle places of pilgrimage in England. Those able to travel further afield strived to journey at least once to Jerusalem and the other places in the Holy Land associated with Jesus, his followers (the disciples of the New Testament), and his predecessors (the prophets of the Old Testament).

It is likely that the first Carmelites were pilgrims who had made such a journey. They were hermits who took their name from Mount Carmel, a mountain ridge overlooking the Mediterranean Sea. Since the ninth century before Christ, Mount Carmel had been regarded as a holy place because it was here that the Old Testament prophet Elijah had proved the supremacy of the one true God of Israel over the false god Baal (as recounted in the Bible's *Books of the Kings*). Since the time of Elijah Carmel had been revered as a place of beauty and fertility between the desert and the sea, Carmel being a Hebrew word that means 'garden', 'vineyard' or 'orchard'. The fertility of Carmel's little valleys and caves was fed by wells and springs, such as the ancient Spring or Fountain of Elijah which remains there today. Sometime at the beginning of the thirteenth century Christian hermits gathered together in a community around this Spring for prayer and mutual support. To guide them in their development they approached the local bishop, Saint Albert of Jerusalem, and asked him to approve their way of life. He did so, issuing a short but profound document which has become known as the *Rule of Saint Albert*. It is this text which inspires Carmelites to this day.

The community of hermits on Mount Carmel shared lives of work and prayer (especially the Mass, Divine Office, and meditating upon the Bible). However, their community was threatened by the continuing Crusader wars. And so in the 1230s they began to leave the Holy Land and migrate to Western Europe. Carmel was for them no longer only a physical place, but a spirit in the heart.

The Carmelites came to England in 1242 and Aylesford was the second hermitage they established (after Hulne in Northumberland). Since the reign of King William II there had been a manor house in Aylesford beside the River Medway, belonging to Baron Richard de Grey. When he returned from the Crusades he brought Carmelites with him and gave them land in Aylesford where they could live out their vocation.

From its origins on Mount Carmel the Carmelite Order has spread throughout the world, but Aylesford holds a special place in the heart of all Carmelites because it was here that a decision was made which had a fundamental impact on the nature of Carmelite life (sometimes called simply 'Carmel'). In 1247 Carmelites from across Europe gathered for a General Chapter. This was a meeting of hermits from different communities around Europe and those who had remained in the Holy Land. At this Chapter the Carmelites petitioned the Pope, Innocent IV, to modify their *Rule of Saint Albert* so that they could found houses in towns and cities as well as in solitary places. Life as hermits had been hard for the Carmelites in Western Europe; it was not so easy to live off the land as it had been on Mount Carmel, and the growth of towns and cities showed the hermits that there was a real need for people living in urban poverty to be brought the Good News of the Gospel.

The result of the General Chapter in Aylesford was that the Carmelites went from being hermits to become mendicant (begging) friars like the Franciscans and Dominicans. Aylesford was a place of rebirth for the Order, which was of great service to the Church. For this reason Aylesford is sometimes called 'the second Carmel'. As friars (which simply means 'brothers') the Carmelites were able to establish houses in towns and cities and go out to encounter God's people. They would offer spiritual advice and share their experience of God with anyone they met, and those brothers who were ordained priests would preach in public places and administer the sacraments.

Eventually there were forty Carmelite friaries (also known as priories or convents) founded in England before the Reformation. There were Carmelite priories in London, Oxford, Cambridge, Ipswich, York, Chester, Bristol, Newcastle, Coventry and many other big urban centres. The Order spread from England to Wales, Scotland and Ireland. The Carmelites became known as *Whitefriars* due to the white cloaks that were worn over their brown habits for preaching and solemn occasions. To this day *Whitefriars Street* in a town is an indication that there was once a Carmelite house on the site.

The Message of Carmel

The Carmelite way of life set out by Saint Albert of Jerusalem and followed by the medieval Carmelites still inspires people today, in Aylesford and throughout the world. Shortly after the Carmelite hermits became friars, lay people were attracted to their shared life of prayer and service. Some of these lay people opted to live the spirit of Carmel within their own homes, giving rise to the lay branch of the Carmelites known as the Third Order. The Carmelite nuns, who are today the best known part of the Carmelite Family, were formalised in the 1400s.

Over centuries of development and reform, Carmelites have formed praying communities at the service of all God's people. The heart of the Carmelite vocation is contemplation, that is, pondering God, fixing our gaze on Jesus, being open and attentive to the Holy Spirit, and doing God's will in our lives. Carmelites are known as contemplatives, that is, people who are open to the in-pouring of God, and this expresses itself in both prayer and service. Carmelites believe that the gift of contemplation is offered to anyone who allows God room in their hearts, so the 'Carmelite Family' consists of not only friars but also nuns, active sisters, hermits, and lay people. They all try to share the Gospel, living 'in allegiance to Jesus Christ' (*Rule of Saint Albert*, Chapter 2).

Fundamental to the message of Carmel is the belief of Elijah that 'God lives, in whose presence I stand' (1 *Kings* 17:1). The message of Carmel is the witness of the prophet Elijah that God is truly God, and the false gods in our lives (such as distorted love of money or power) must be rejected if we are to grow as human beings made in God's image.

The 'message of Carmel', or Carmelite spirituality, is quite simply the way that Carmelites live and approach the Christian Gospel, the Good News revealed through and in Jesus, that God loves us and seeks a deep relationship with us. This relationship is nurtured in prayer, which the great Carmelite saint Teresa of Jesus (of Avila) said is simply 'a close sharing between friends; it means taking time frequently to be alone with him who we know loves us' (*Life* 8, 5).

Carmelites do not have one particular way of praying, though very important is the regular celebration of the Eucharist and the praying of the Divine Office throughout the day whenever possible. Also important is a daily encounter with Jesus, the Word of God, in the Bible. *Lectio Divina* meditation on the Scriptures is a way of life common in many Carmelite communities. As well as praying together, Carmelites spend time in solitude and stillness because they believe that God speaks to the heart most clearly in silence, as he did to Elijah on Mount Horeb (1 *Kings* 19).

Just as there is no single 'Carmelite method' of prayer, so there is no single form of Carmelite ministry or service. Carmelites blend prayer with active service of those around them, and this takes many different forms depending on the time and the place Carmelites find themselves in.

Like all the ancient religious orders (such as the Benedictines, Franciscans and Jesuits), Carmelites have developed a distinctive way of living the Gospel that is particular for them, with their own traditions, imagery, language, and spiritual landscape. This is sometimes called the Carmelite 'charism', that is, the particular gifts that God has given to the Carmelite Family for the service of the Church and the World.

The Carmelite pilgrimage through life has been well trodden by many holy women and men. With the saints of Carmel we look for union with God and strive for eternal salvation. Over the centuries 'Carmel' has produced some of the greatest Christian thinkers, mystics, and philosophers, such as Teresa of Jesus (of Avila), John of the Cross, and Thérèse of Lisieux (three Carmelite 'Doctors of the Church'). In the twentieth century, the Carmelite Family bore witness to the Gospel in the martyrdoms of Titus Brandsma, Teresa Benedicta of the Cross (Edith Stein), and Isidore Bakanja.

Today there are communities of Carmelite and Discalced Carmelite friars, nuns, sisters and laypeople across England, Scotland, and Wales. Similar communities exist in Ireland, and throughout the world. Together they make up the wider 'Carmelite Family' which seeks the face of the Living God in parishes, prisons, university chaplaincies, retreat centres, workplaces, schools, and through many other forms of ministry.

The decision taken by the hermits at Aylesford in 1247 to adapt to new situations has had far-reaching consequences. Perhaps that is why so many people come to Aylesford for guidance at the cross-roads of life.

Aylesford Today

Aylesford is a particularly important and much-loved place in the memory of the Carmelite Family, and for the many people who visit it without knowing its historical significance. Today it is a venue for sharing the message of Carmel with the thousands of visitors who visit The Friars each year.

Having been closed as a religious community at the Reformation, the medieval buildings became a private residence known as The Friars, a name which the Priory has retained (although these days people with various Carmelite vocations live on the site alongside the brothers).

The Friars is a collection of medieval and modern buildings. The original chapel, destroyed to construct other edifices, was dedicated to the Assumption of Our Lady the Blessed Virgin Mary into Heaven. This would have been the heart of the medieval community.

The oldest building to have survived is the Pilgrim's Hall in the Great Courtyard which dates back to 1280. It was built to accommodate pilgrims and guests, many of whom were on their way to the shrine of St Thomas Becket at Canterbury. Some would have dined in the Prior's Hall where today paintings relate the Carmelite story.

In the medieval friary the Cloisters were the area where the brothers could walk, talk, work and pray. Two sides of the original Cloisters remain and leading off them is the Cloister Chapel, the only public chapel in the surviving medieval buildings. Inside is a small shrine to St Jude and a stained-glass window depicting Our Lady as the *Flos Carmeli* (Flower of Carmel). This window was a gift from the artist, Moira Forsyth, who was received into the Catholic Church in the Cloister Chapel. The chapel also houses a statue of the Infant of Prague from the Carmelite church in that city.

When the Carmelite friars returned to their ancient home in 1949, many people came on pilgrimage from far and wide to visit the largely ruined buildings. The friars had not expected Aylesford to become a place of pilgrimage, but the desire of the people was so strong that under the charismatic leadership of the Prior, Fr Malachy Lynch, the brethren decided to build a shrine and dedicate it - like the medieval chapel - to Our Lady of the Assumption. Our Lady's Assumption (her rising body and soul to Heaven) had been defined as a dogma (official teaching) of the Church in 1950. The present Shrine was built in the late 1950s upon the site of the original medieval Church (which is outlined by coloured paving slabs on the piazza in front). Many artists, builders and volunteers worked to build what Fr Malachy called 'a prayer in stone'. The altars at the Shrine were consecrated in 1965.

The Shrine

During the summer there are frequent outdoor Masses and other religious services, with individuals and pilgrim groups coming from Kent, London, and beyond. They come by car, coach, train, bike, and on foot. Particular highlights include pilgrimages for the Tamil community, Altar Servers, Polish Scouts and Guides, the Union of Catholic Mothers, the Knights of Saint Columba, the Nigerian pilgrimage, the Italian pilgrimage, diocesan pilgrimages, days for religious, school groups and the Little Flower Society. Around the feast of the Shrine (15th August) the Pilgrimage of the Sick allows participants to receive the Sacrament of Anointing. The feast day of Our Lady of Mount Carmel (16th July) is another very important date in the calendar, particularly for Lay Carmelites (members of the Third Order) who travel from across Britain to renew their profession promises. Many non-Catholics come to Aylesford for prayer and peace, making it a centre for ecumenical and interfaith encounter. With pilgrims coming from different places and cultural backgrounds, Aylesford truly lives up to its ancient name which means 'a crossing place for all people'.

The outdoor shrine is dominated by the statue of the Glorious Assumption of Our Lady by the sculptor Michael Clark. Maintaining a medieval tradition, the friars process to this statue every Saturday evening in the summer months to keep the 'Saturday Station', a series of prayers and hymns in honour of Mary. (The words can be found in the prayers at the back of this booklet).

On either side of the outdoor Shrine are chapels dedicated to Mary's husband St Joseph, and her mother St Anne. In the former the stories of St Joseph and the prophet St Elijah are told through the medium of striking ceramics made by the Polish artist Adam Kossowski (d. 1987) whose work can be seen throughout the shrine. Kossowski's works were an act of thanksgiving for his release from a slave labour camp in Russia. In the St Anne Chapel is a beautiful medieval statue of the saint holding both Mary and Jesus as infants, and this spot is dedicated to prayer for families. Opposite St Joseph's is the Choir Chapel which in keeping with Carmelite values is kept simple and is used daily by the Carmelite community for Mass, the Divine Office, the Rosary, Benediction and other liturgies.

The biggest chapel, leading off from the outdoor Shrine, is the Relic Chapel where Mass is celebrated every Sunday of the year. It is so called because it houses the relics of St Simon Stock, a Prior General (senior brother) of the Carmelites in the Middle Ages. In 1951 his skull was given to The Friars by the Archbishop of Bordeaux, where Simon had been buried. It rests just behind the altar in a reliquary that symbolises Mount Carmel. It is constantly surrounded by burning candles which pilgrims light to prolong their prayer. Their radiance mingles with light from the magnificent windows by Fr Louis Norris O.S.B., a Benedictine monk from Buckfast Abbey in Devon. Also in the Relic Chapel are two side chapels: one dedicated to the martyrs of England and Wales, and the other to the holy men and women of the Carmelite Family. In the middle of the ceramics of the Carmelite saints there is an antique Flemish statue of Our Lady of Mount Carmel. On special occasions this is carried in procession around the Rosary Way.

The Rosary Way is located behind the main Shrine, a place of peace and prayer where pilgrims can stroll through beautiful gardens alongside the River Medway whilst meditating on the mysteries of the Rosary which are depicted in ceramic by Adam Kossowski. At the entrance to the Rosary Way is the Gatehouse of the medieval friary, behind which a Peace Garden is being developed. This will allow pilgrims to reflect upon the beauty of God's creation, as will the woodland walk which was planted to mark the millennium.

At the entrance to The Friars stand two restored seventeenth century barns. One is used as a tearoom and gift/book-shop, whilst the other is a welcome centre dedicated to Saint Teresa Benedicta of the Cross (Edith Stein). There is still a working pottery in the grounds and visitors are welcome to watch experienced potters at work.

Although many visitors to Aylesford come for just the day - often picnicking by the duck pond or in the grounds - a good number stay overnight in the medieval guesthouse. As well as having access to the Pilgrims' Hall for meals, these guests can gain spiritual nourishment by visiting the Pilgrims' Library on the first floor of the Hall. Some pilgrims who come to Aylesford overnight do so for the monthly Prayer Vigils which last from dusk till dawn.

Many of the pilgrims who come to Aylesford - and even those who have not - keep in touch with the Shrine through the Newsletter which is sent out four times a year by the Carmelite Prior. The Newsletter Office is located in the Conference Centre which offers meeting rooms and resources for visiting groups. Some of the groups using the Centre are secular in nature, drawn to Aylesford by its sense of peace and beauty. However, its most important work is the series of retreats, talks and spiritual events that are organised throughout the year. Also operating throughout the year is a counselling service.

Spread across the medieval and modern buildings are offices for the Carmelite community and staff who work at Aylesford. Amongst these are the information office for those seeking to know more about the Lay Carmelite vocation, and the various sacristies for the different chapels.

The friars at Aylesford are always available to talk with visitors, share their stories, listen to their problems, and support them with their prayers.

Mary in the Carmelite Tradition

Anyone who visits Aylesford, or indeed any other Carmelite community, will be struck by the particular love and devotion which Carmelites have for Mary the Mother of God, Our Lady. Of course, Carmelites are not unique in this - many Christians love Our Lady - but for the Carmelite Family this devotion goes back to its very beginnings and says something important about Carmelite identity.

The medieval Carmelites living near the Spring of Elijah on Mount Carmel dedicated their chapel to Mary whom they called 'The Lady of the Place'. Mary and the prophet Elijah are seen as models for the Carmelite way or life and an integral part of the Order's charism. However, neither Mary, Elijah, nor Saint Albert are regarded today as the founders of the Order. Rather Mary is held in esteem as the Patron of the Order, our Mother, our Sister, the Virgin Most Pure, and the Beauty of Carmel.

Mary is not mentioned explicitly in the *Rule* given by St Albert of Jerusalem to the hermit brothers on Mount Carmel. However, some have seen allusion to Mary in Chapter 10 of the *Rule* that mentions the chapel that was to be built and which was later dedicated to her. There are

The Great Courtyard at The Friars, Aylesford

parallels between the *Rule of Saint Albert* and the legislation of other institutes of monks and canons which were notable for their Marian dimension. The fact that Mary is not always mentioned in their founding documents is not because Mary was dismissed but because the religious culture of the day saw Mary as a model and inspiration in every aspect of life, a woman who embodied what it is to follow Jesus.

Mary in the Carmelite Rule

To illustrate this, a great medieval theologian called John Baconthorpe (d. 1348) sought to show how Mary was the perfect model for how Carmelites should live. In a commentary on the Carmelite *Rule*, Baconthorpe showed Carmelites how Mary was a fundamental part of their lives, even from the time of Elijah who predated her. For example, in the Old Testament story of Elijah (1 *Kings* 18:44) the prophet saw a small cloud rising from the sea which would bring rain to Israel after a long drought. Inspired by an ancient tradition of the Fathers of the Church, Baconthorpe said that the small cloud was a symbol of Mary. Just as the cloud brought rain to restore the fruitfulness of the earth after the long drought, so Mary brought Jesus to the people of Israel, whose grace would restore humanity to a right relationship with God: 'The love of God descended on Mary…and through Mary the rains of mercy and grace descended on what was dried up, and thus restored all things.'

John Baconthorpe's *Commentary on the Carmelite Rule* makes creative comparisons between Mary's life as we see it in the Gospel with elements of Carmelite life as we see it in the *Rule of Saint Albert*. For instance, the *Rule* requires each hermit to have a separate cell; this is like Mary, who was found contemplating in her own private room by the angel Gabriel. The *Rule* says that a chapel is to be built in the middle of the hermits' cells; in like manner Mary was brought from her private room by her parents to the central place of Jewish worship, the Temple. Just as Saint Albert says that the Carmelite is to remain meditating in or near his cell when not otherwise lawfully occupied, so Mary prayed for many hours each day when not doing her duties. The *Rule* encourages the Carmelite to cultivate silence so that he can hear the word of God; Mary speaks no more than four times in the Gospel accounts, pondering God's word in her heart. The *Rule of Saint Albert* says that Carmelites may keep asses and mule (rather than horses); in comparison Mary rode a humble ass to Bethlehem. The Prior is required by the *Rule* to serve the other members of the community, just as Mary stayed with her cousin Elizabeth and cared for her for three months.

Although a somewhat quaint document to modern tastes, John Baconthorpe's *Commentary* shows an early desire within the Order for the Carmelites to pattern their lives on Mary, the Mother of Jesus. The Order soon became known as the *Brothers of Our Lady of Mount Carmel*, the first reference to this being a papal document in 1252. The Carmelites argued that if they were the 'brothers of Our Lady of Mount Carmel', then Mary was their sister. They claimed to have a particularly close relationship with Mary, and looked on her with the intimacy and affection of an elder sister, as well as Mother and Queen. Centuries later Pope Paul VI would call Mary 'our older sister in the faith'. Not everyone feels comfortable calling Mary their sister, but to do so does not lower Mary to our level; rather it raises us to hers and reminds us that she is first among us, the children of God. Mary remains a sign of liberation and freedom for all who cry to God in their need.

Although Mary is not mentioned frequently in early Carmelite documents, she is a constant presence in the background. In 1282 a Prior General of the Carmelites, Peter Millau, wrote a letter to the King of England, Edward I, asking him to protect the Order, which he said was under the special patronage of Mary. Patronage was a special relationship of trust and mutual obligation in the medieval world; Mary protected and promoted her Order, and in return its members promised her faithful love and service.

When the Carmelites came together for a General Chapter meeting in 1287 they further defined their understanding of the Marian nature of the Order, stating that it was founded specifically for the honour and glory of Mary.

In the Middle Ages as today, the principles of day-to-day Carmelite life were set out in the *Rule of Saint Albert*, but the practicalities were elaborated in guidelines called the *Constitutions*. It was not until 1324 that Mary is mentioned in the introductory text of the Order's *Constitutions* which states: 'After the incarnation the Carmelites built a church on Mount Carmel in honour of the Blessed Virgin Mary, and chose her title. Therefore from that time they were, by apostolic privilege, called the Brothers of the Blessed Virgin Mary of Mount Carmel.' This document taught young novices why their Order was closely linked to Mary, and over subsequent years the different titles the Carmelites gave her shows their developing sense of Our Lady's closeness, protection, and love. In the *Constitutions* issued in 1586 we read that the full title of the Order had become *The Brothers of the Order of the Most Blessed Mother of God the Virgin Mary of Mount Carmel*. This emphasised Mary's role as both sister to Carmelites, Mother of God, and a woman of purity.

As well as recognising Mary's physical purity, the Carmelite tradition of calling Our Lady 'the Most Pure Virgin' recognises that she is pure in heart. Her responsiveness at the Annunciation shows that Mary only sought to allow God's will in her life. Nothing distracted her from God. As Most Pure Virgin Mary is an inspiration to all who follow her example of a chaste life given over to God. She practiced what Carmelites call *vacare Deo* or 'making space for God'.

Inspiration of the charism

One of the most important spiritual writings in the Carmelite tradition is a document called *The Ten Books on the Way of Life and Great Deeds of the Carmelites*, better known as *The Institution of the First Monks*. The *Ten Books* is not a history of the Carmelites in the modern sense but rather a spiritual and symbolic reflection on the Order's charism. The work was compiled around the year 1385 by Philip Ribot, the Prior Provincial of the Carmelites in Catalonia, north of Spain. At first it was thought to have been written much earlier, perhaps parts even as early as the fourth century, but it is now agreed that it only goes back in its present form to the fourteenth century. Most of *The Ten Books* presents Elijah as the model for the religious life, but Book Six deals with Mary. Like John Baconthorpe, Philip Ribot reflects upon the significance of the cloud seen by Elijah rising from the sea: 'The key to its Marian symbolism is that the cloud of pure rain, that is Mary, arose from the bitter salty sea, which is the image of sinful humanity'. Just as the cloud was pure water arising from the salty ocean, so Mary was a pure woman preserved from the sinfulness of humanity through her Immaculate Conception.

Today pilgrims to Aylesford still look to Mary as a source of inspiration and intercession. She is a tender mother who stands with us in times of joy and pain, just as she is seen at the wedding in Cana, and at the foot of the cross. Carmelites and people who like to pray with them can follow Mary's guidance towards her son: 'Do whatever he tells you' (*Luke* 2:5). Mary was the first teacher and first follower of Jesus. She shows us how to listen to the Word of God in scripture, to be open to the needs of others in a world where there is so much poverty.

Carmelites use Mount Carmel as an image of the spiritual journey, a pilgrimage through life. As we climb the mountain towards its summit, Jesus Christ, there will be parts of the route that are smooth and easy, and parts that are more rocky and difficult. Mary, Our Lady of Mount Carmel, can lead us up the mountain to meet her son Jesus. Like an older sister, Mary is the one who walks with us upon the pilgrim path. She has trodden the road before us, and where Mary has been, we will follow.

Mary and the Carmelite Scapular

The Carmelite Family has promoted one of the most popular devotions within the Church: the wearing of the brown scapular. The scapular consists of two small pieces of brown cloth, joined together with cord, that is worn over the shoulders (the word *scapular* derives from the Latin for 'shoulder blade'). The scapular developed in the Renaissance as a miniature version of the religious habit. It became particularly popular amongst lay people who wanted to have a discreet but visible sign of identifying with the Carmelite way of life.

The scapular, like all devotions to Mary, should lead us closer to her son Jesus. The scapular is still an important 'sacramental' leading us to Christ, and can be worn by any Christian. Part of the ministry of the friars at Aylesford is to 'enrol' people in the brown scapular, thus incorporating them into the great Carmelite Family. The scapular is seen as a sign of Mary's care and protection of the whole Carmelite Family. The scapular was first mentioned in the Carmelite *Constitutions* of 1281, but it did not become popular among lay people until centuries later when it became seen as Mary's own special habit. In the late Middle Ages accounts emerged of Our Lady having appeared in a vision to Saint Simon Stock while at prayer, promising special protection to the Carmelites, and that the scapular of their religious habit would be a sign of that protection. In the Middle Ages people could show their allegiance to a lord or lady by the clothes they wore; the scapular showed to the world the Carmelites' allegiance to Mary and her son.

Simon Stock was an early Prior General of the Order and was possibly elected at the General Chapter held in London in 1254. He was thus Prior General during the period when the Carmelites were changing from being hermits to friars. There are different traditions about where the vision of Our Lady to Simon Stock supposedly took place, with Aylesford or Cambridge proposed as possible sites. Tradition says that St Simon Stock wrote a hymn to Our Lady called the *Flos Carmeli* (the Flower of Carmel). It is still sung by Carmelites around the world, and two verses can be found in the prayers at the back of this booklet. Simon may have come from Kent, either from Stoke near the Isle of Grain, or Stockbury near Sittingbourne. His family seems to have had links with France, and he died in Bordeaux in 1261, where he was buried in the Cathedral. In 1951 some of the relics of St Simon Stock were brought to England by the Archbishop of Bordeaux and are now at Aylesford in the appropriately named Relic Chapel.

Detail of the Scapular Vision Shrine ceramic

There is very little hard evidence about the origin of the scapular vision story. Whatever the historical facts, the scapular vision story tells us important truths about the close relationship between Mary and the Carmelite Family. The Carmelites look upon Mary as their patron and protector; a mother who clothes her children, wrapping them in a mantle of love. The scapular reminds us that Mary is a sure guide to those who seek God. It is no magic charm but rather a sign of our confidence in Mary's care in life and in death. Those of us who wear the scapular must 'put on' Mary's attitudes and clothe ourselves with her virtues. The scapular was originally an apron worn by friars to protect their habits, so when we put it on it can be a reminder of how we are called to work for God's kingdom, and seek - like Mary - to be of humble service to God through our neighbour. After being enrolled in the scapular by a Carmelite there are no particular prayers attached to the scapular, though many say "Mary, use me in the service of your son today" when putting it on. Rather than being associated with particular prayers, the scapular invites us to make all life a prayer and is a sign that we have 'put on Christ' (*Galatians* 3:27).

Pope John Paul II and Oscar Romero (the martyred Archbishop of El Salvador) both wore the brown scapular. There is even a martyr for the scapular, Blessed Isidore Bakanja (1887-1909). He was a labourer in Zaire who encouraged his fellow workers, who were treated like slaves by their colonial overlords, to become Christian. He was beaten and left to die for preaching about Christ and refusing to take off the scapular. Before he died he forgave his murderer. He certainly took the message of the scapular to heart.

In Aylesford the scapular vision story is commemorated by a shrine altar on the Rosary Way, which contains earth brought from near the Spring of Elijah on Mount Carmel.

Prayers for Pilgrims

Everyone must find their own way of praying to God, their own way of conversing with the friend who we know loves us. Sometimes we pray with the Bible, sometimes we ask the saints to pray with us, sometimes we pray in silence. Pilgrims who come to Aylesford often like to pray with the Carmelite community as well as on their own, so we offer here some prayers derived from the Carmelite tradition.

Prayer before a pilgrimage

Loving and merciful God,
when Abraham and Sarah left their own land,
you kept them safe.
You led the children of Israel on dry land,
parting the waters of the Red Sea.
You guided the Magi to your Son by a star.
Help us, your children,
that we may reach our destination in safety
and return home safe to our families and loved ones.
And when life's journey is over,
welcome us to our heavenly home.
We ask this through Christ our Lord. Amen.

Prayer in the spirit and power of Elijah

This prayer might be particularly suitable before the ceramics of Elijah in the St Joseph Chapel at Aylesford.

O Lord, the God of Abraham, Isaac and Israel,
You alone are God.
Your servant Elijah lived in your presence,
and acted on your Word.
Help us to drink from the well of his wisdom.
Shelter us in Cherith, and lead us to Carmel,
luring our hearts away from all false gods.
Open our eyes to the needs of those suffering.
Open our mouths to speak comfort and justice.
Open our hearts to your voice in the silence.
Send angels to strengthen us.
Send the rain of your grace to quench our thirst.
Let us break bread with the starving
and bring life to places of death and despair.
Send us as prophets to herald your Gospel.
Allow us to rise to you in paradise.
Those who met your son Jesus saw in him
the spirit of Elijah.
May Elijah lead us to your son.
We ask this in Jesus' name. Amen.

Prayer for our homes and those whom we love

This might be a particularly suitable prayer in the Saint Anne Chapel at Aylesford.

O God, Father and Mother to us,
by whose will we live together in families and communities,
let your blessing rest upon our homes and those we love.
Bless our parents, the members of our families,
our friends and those we care for.
Give them health and strength of soul and body,
and unite us all in love of you.
Through Christ our Lord. Amen.

Prayer for vocations to the religious life and priesthood

This might be a particularly suitable prayer in the Choir Chapel at Aylesford.

O Lord Jesus Christ, who has said -
"The harvest indeed is great but the labourers are few.
Pray therefore to the Lord of the harvest
that he may send labourers into his harvest" -
grant to members in our society the gift of
a vocation to the religious life and priesthood.
Grant them the grace to accept your invitation and
the strength to fulfil their vocation
that they may do great things for God
and the salvation of the human family.

Call men and women to the Carmelite Family,
both religious and laypeople.
And as all of us are called to be a royal priesthood,
help us work - in whatever way is pleasing to you -
to build up the Kingdom of Heaven. Amen.

Prayer for Christian Unity

This might be a particularly suitable prayer in the Chapel of the Martyrs of England and Wales at Aylesford.

Lord Jesus Christ,
you prayed that your followers should be one,
as you and your Father are one.
We are sorry for the scandal of division between the Christian Churches.
Help us to celebrate our diverse gifts and insights,
so that we may be united as one rainbow is made of many colours.
Help us live the Gospel together,
so that in East and West, North and South,
others may see how Christians love one another. Amen.

Act of Sorrow

You might like to pray this outside the confessionals by the main Shrine at Aylesford.

O my God, I thank you for loving me.
I am sorry for all my sins,
for not loving others and not loving you.
Help me to live like Jesus and not sin again. Amen.

Prayer to Saint Simon Stock

This might be a particularly suitable prayer in the Relic Chapel at The Friars.

Heavenly Father, you called Saint Simon Stock to serve you in the brotherhood of Our Lady of Mount Carmel.
Through his prayers, help us - like him - to live in your presence,
and to work for the salvation of the human family.
We ask this through Christ our Lord. Amen.

Litany of Saint Joseph

This might be particularly suitable for prayer in the St Joseph Chapel at Aylesford.

Lord, have mercy, *Christ, have mercy,*
Lord, have mercy, *Holy Trinity, One God, have mercy on us.*
Holy Mary, *Pray for us.* St Joseph, *(repeat)*
Renowncd offspring of David,
Spouse of the Mother of God,
Foster father of the Son of God,
Diligent protector of the Holy Family,
Joseph most just,
Joseph most chaste,
Mirror of patience,
Lover of poverty,
Model of workers,
Pillar of families,
Solace of the sick and dying,
Protector of God's holy Church,
Principal protector of the Carmelite Order.

Let us pray:
Father God, you were pleased to choose blessed Joseph
to be the spouse of your obedient daughter Mary,
and foster father of your divine Son.
Grant, we beg you, that through his intercession and example,
our homes may be worthy of Christ,
in whose name we make this prayer. Amen.

Prayer to Saint Anne

This prayer would be particularly appropriate in the Saint Anne Chapel at Aylesford.

Good Saint Anne,
you were especially favoured by God
to be the mother of the most holy Virgin Mary,
and thus grandmother of our Saviour Jesus Christ.
By your intimacy with your most pure daughter and her divine Son,
kindly obtain for us the graces that we seek.
Secure for us the strength to perform faithfully our daily duties
and the help we need to persevere in the love of Jesus and Mary. Amen.

Prayer to the Saints of Carmel

This might be particularly suitable for prayer in the Carmelite Saints Chapel.

Holy men and women of Carmel,
you found in the Carmelite Family a school of prayer,
a community ready to serve others,
and sure companions for your pilgrimage through life.
From your place at the summit of Mount Carmel,
Jesus Christ, help us to walk steadily in his footsteps,
that our prayers and good works may further the cause of his Church. Amen.

Prayer for the Carmelite Family

This prayer might be particularly suitable in the piazza before the main Shrine of Our Lady of the Assumption at Aylesford.

Tender-hearted God,
renew the gift of the Holy Spirit
within the Carmelite Family
as we seek to live following
in the footsteps of Jesus Christ.
Teach us, like Mary, to contemplate your wisdom.
Fill us, like Elijah, with zeal for your glory.
Inspire us, like Simon Stock,
to ponder your will in times of change.
Like Teresa, John, Thérèse and Titus,
may we live always in your presence,
and make us prophets of your Kingdom.
May our lives of prayer, community, and service
be a sign to the world that God lives,
in whose presence we stand.
This grace we ask in Jesus' name. Amen.

Prayers to Our Lady

Some of the most ancient and beautiful Christian prayers are addressed to the Mother of God. None, however, surpasses Mary's own great canticle, the Magnificat, which is the inspiration of many prayers to Our Lady. Here is a selection of the best known Marian prayers, and lesser known prayers from the Carmelite tradition that speak of Mary as Queen, Mother, Patron, Sister, and Beauty of Carmel.

The Magnificat
(The Canticle of Mary - Luke 1:46-55)

This might be a particularly suitable prayer before the main Shrine of Our Lady of the Assumption at Aylesford.

My soul glorifies the Lord,
my spirit rejoices in God, my Saviour.
He looks on his servant in her lowliness;
henceforth all ages will call me blessed.
The Almighty works marvels for me.
Holy his name!
His mercy is from age to age,
on those who fear him.
He puts forth his arm in strength
and scatters the proud-hearted.

He casts the mighty from their thrones
and raises the lowly.
He fills the starving with good things,
sends the rich away empty.
He protects Israel, his servant,
remembering his mercy,
the mercy promised to our forebears,
to Abraham and his line for ever.

Ave Maria (Hail Mary)

Hail Mary, full of grace,
the Lord is with you.
Blessed are you among women,
and blessed is the fruit of your womb, Jesus.
Holy Mary, Mother of God,
pray for us sinners now,
and at the hour of our death. Amen.

Flos Carmeli (Flower of Carmel)

This might be a particularly suitable prayer in the Cloister Chapel at Aylesford.

Flower of Carmel,
Tall vine, blossom laden,
Splendour of heaven,
Child-bearing, yet maiden,
None equals thee.

Mother so tender,
Whom no man didst know,
On Carmel's children
Thy favour bestow.
Star of the Sea.

V. Holy Mary, Mother of Christ, hear the cry of your servants.
R. And bring down heavenly aid in answer to our prayer.

Let us pray:

By a special privilege, Lord,
you have adorned the Carmelite Order
with the name of your Mother,
the most glorious Virgin Mary.
Grant as we faithfully remember this honour,
that in these days we may receive her protection
and in the days to come we may be brought
to everlasting happiness.
This we ask of you who are living and reigning for ever.
Amen.

Verses to Our Lady of Mount Carmel

V. Blessed Virgin of Mount Carmel;
R. Be our constant hope.

V. Mary, perfect disciple of the Lord;
R. Make us also faithful to him.

V. Mary, Flower of Carmel;
R. Fill us with your joy.

V. Virgin Mary, beauty of Carmel;
R. Smile upon your family.

V. Gentle Mother of Carmel;
R. Embrace me as your child.

V. Mary, Mother beyond compare
R. Remember your children forever.

V. Holy Virgin, Star of the Sea;
R. Be our beacon of light.

V. Protecting Veil;
R. Shelter us in the mantle of your love.

V. Mary, conceived without sin;
R. Pray for us who have recourse to you.

Let us pray:

O Father of all, look upon us as your children,
and support us with your strength.
May we, who honour the memory of
Our Lady of Mount Carmel,
always rejoice in her unfailing protection.
Through Christ our Lord. Amen.

Acclamations in honour of the Mother of Christ

Mary the Dawn - Christ the Perfect Day;
Mary the Gate - Christ the Heavenly Way!
Mary the Root - Christ the Mystic Vine;
Mary the Grape - Christ the Sacred Wine!
Mary the Stem - Christ the Rose, blood-red;
Mary the Wheat - Christ the Living Bread!
Mary the Fount - Christ the Cleansing Flood;
Mary the Cup - Christ the Saving Blood!
Mary the Temple - Christ the Temple's Lord;
Mary the Shrine - Christ the God adored!
Mary the Beacon - Christ the heaven's Rest;
Mary the Mirror - Christ the Vision Blest!
Mary the Mother - Christ the Mother's Son;
By all things bless'd while endless ages run!

Prayer before an Image of Our Lady of Mount Carmel

O God, you have given us Mary as our Mother
and through the Order of Carmel
we learn to call her sister.
May we imitate her goodness and faith,
and be ever joyful in the wonderful things
you have done for us.
May Mary watch over and protect us
on our pilgrim way to your holy mountain, Christ the Lord.
We make our prayer through the same Christ, our Lord.
Amen.

(Terenure College, Dublin, Ireland)

Salve Regina (Hail, Holy Queen)

Hail, Holy Queen, Mother of Mercy,
hail our life our sweetness and our hope.
To you do we cry, poor banished children of Eve;
to you do we send up our sighs, mourning
and weeping in this valley of tears.
Turn then most gracious advocate,
your eyes of mercy towards us;
and after this our exile,
show unto us the blessed fruit of your womb, Jesus.
O clement, O loving, O sweet Virgin Mary.

V. Pray for us, O Holy Mother of God.
R. That we may be made worthy of the promises of Christ.

Let us pray:

Protect your servants, Lord, and keep us in peace.
As we trust in the intercession of the
Blessed Virgin Mary and all the saints,
keep us safe from every danger
and bring us to everlasting life
through Christ our Lord.
Amen.

Regina Coeli

(Antiphon to Our Lady for Eastertime)

O Queen of Heaven, rejoice; Alleluia!
For he whom thou didst merit to bear: Alleluia!
Has risen, as he said: Alleluia!
Pray for us to God: Alleluia!

V. Rejoice and be glad, O Virgin Mary:
R. For the Lord has risen indeed, Alleluia!

Let us pray:

O God, who through the resurrection of thy Son,
Our Lord, Jesus Christ,
was pleased to give joy to the world,
grant we beseech you,
that like his mother, the Virgin Mary,
we may obtain the joys of everlasting life.
Amen.

Memorare

Remember, O most gracious Virgin Mary,
that never was it known that anyone,
who fled to your protection,
implored your help, or sought your intercession,
was left unaided.
Inspired by this confidence,
I fly to you, O virgin of virgins my Mother.
To you do I come,
before you I stand, sinful and sorrowful.
O Mother of the Word incarnate, despise not my petitions,
but in your clemency, hear and answer me. Amen.

The Carmelite 'Saturday Station'

*This is prayed at Aylesford Priory each Saturday after
Night Prayer. After an antiphon to Our Lady (such as the
Salve Regina or Regina Coeli) the following prayer is said:*

Almighty Father of our Lord Jesus Christ,
you have revealed the beauty of your power by exalting
the lowly maiden of Nazareth and making her
the Mother of our Saviour.
May the prayers of this woman, clothed with the sun,
and with the moon beneath her feet,
bring Jesus to the waiting world
and fill the hearts of all with the presence of her child,
who lives and reigns for ever and ever. Amen.

The asperges (sprinkling with water) follows as a Psalm is prayed:

Antiphon: Purify me, Lord, with hyssop until I am clean; wash me and I shall be whiter than snow.

Psalm: Have mercy on me, God in your kindness, in your compassion blot out my offence.

Indeed you love truth in the heart; then in the secret of my heart teach me wisdom.

Glory be to the Father…

Antiphon: Purify me, Lord, with hyssop until I am clean; wash me and I shall be whiter than snow.

V. Lord, show us your mercy and love.
R. And grant us your salvation.

Let us pray:

O Lord, holy Father, almighty and eternal God,
hear us, and in your kindness
send your holy angel from heaven to guide,
support, protect, visit and defend all those
who live in this house.
We ask this in the name of Christ, our Lord. Amen.
Prior: May the faithful departed, through the mercy of God,
rest in peace. Amen.

The Flos Carmeli (Flower of Carmel) is now said or sung.

V. Holy Mary, Mother of Christ, hear the cry of your servants.
R. And bring down heavenly aid in answer to our prayer.

V. Lord, hear my prayer.
R. And let my cry come unto you.
V. The Lord be with you.
R. And also with you.

Let us pray:

By a special priviledge, Lord,
you have adorned our Order with the name of your mother,
the most glorious Virgin Mary:
as we faithfully remember this honour
grant that in these days we may receive her protection,
and in the days to come be brought, through her prayers,
to the joy of heaven.
And we ask this of you who live and reign for ever and
ever. Amen.

V. May the blessed Virgin Mary help us in every trial and
danger.
R. Amen.
V. May God grant us peace.
R. And everlasting life. Amen.

Dedication to Mary, our Mother

Pray for us ever, Holy Mother of God.
Pray for us, whatever be our cross,
as we pass along our way.
Pray for us, and we shall rise again,
though we have fallen.
Pray for us when sorrow,
anxiety or sickness comes upon us.
Pray for us when we are prostrate
under the power of temptation.   *(Cardinal Newman)*

Our guiding star

When the storm of temptation arises,
when you are amidst the reefs and shoals of tribulation,
fix your gaze on the Star of the Sea.
Call upon Mary.

Do the billows of anger, of avarice, of lust
batter against your soul - invoke her name.
In perils and sorrows and fears
fix your gaze on the Star of the Sea.
Call upon Mary.

Under her protection, you shall know no fear.
Under her guidance, you shall not falter.
Under her patronage, you shall reach your goal.
Fix your gaze on the Star of the Sea.
Call upon Mary.
                              (St Bernard)

The Angelus

A traditional prayer for morning, noon and evening

V. The angel of the Lord declared unto Mary:
R. And she conceived by the Holy Spirit.
Hail Mary...

V. Behold the handmaid of the Lord:
R. Be it done to me according to your word.
Hail Mary...

V. And the Word was made flesh:
R. And dwelt among us.
Hail Mary...

V. Pray for us, O holy mother of God.
R. That we may be made worthy of the promises of Christ.

Let us pray:

Pour forth, we beseech you, O Lord,
your grace into our hearts,
that we to whom the incarnation of Christ, your Son,
was made known by the message of an angel,
may by his passion and cross
be brought to the glory of his resurrection,
through the same Christ our Lord. Amen.

The Rosary

The Rosary is an ancient pattern of prayer popular among Christians. At heart it is a series of mediations on some aspects - or 'mysteries' - of the life of Jesus and his mother Mary. The full Rosary is made up of praying four sets of five mysteries, though normally only one set of mysteries is prayed at one sitting (a 'chaplet'). Meditation on each mystery is accompanied by the praying of the Lord's Prayer, followed by ten 'Hail Mary's', concluding with one 'Glory be'. There can also be a space for private reflection. You might like to pray as you walk along the Rosary Way in Aylesford.

The Joyful Mysteries

The Annunciation of the Lord·
  Be it done unto me according to your word. (Luke 1:38)

The Visitation of the Virgin Mary to Elizabeth
  My soul magnifies the Lord. (Luke 1:46)

The Nativity of the Lord
  Peace on earth to those in God's favour. (Luke 2:14)

The Presentation of the Lord
  My eyes have seen your salvation. (Luke 2:30)

The Finding of the Child Jesus in the Temple
  I must be busy with my Father's affairs. (Luke 2:49)

The Mysteries of Light

The Baptism of Jesus in the River Jordan
You are my Son, the Beloved. (Mark 1:11)

The Sign at the Wedding Feast of Cana
His disciples believed in him. (John 2:11)

The Preaching of the Kingdom of Heaven
Repent and believe. (Mark 1:15)

The Transfiguration
It is wonderful for us to be here. (Luke 9:33)

The Institution of the Eucharist
This is my body. (Matthew 26:26)

The Sorrowful Mysteries

The Agony in the Garden
Not my will, but yours, be done. (Matthew 26:39)

The Scourging at the Pillar
First scourged, then handed over to be crucified. (Matthew 27:26)

The Crowning with Thorns
Pilate said: 'Here is the man!' (John 19:5)

The Carrying of the Cross
Do not weep for me; weep rather for yourselves. (Lk 23:28)

The Crucifixion of the Lord
Father, into your hands I commend my spirit. (Luke 23:46)

The Glorious Mysteries

The Resurrection of the Lord
You shall see him, as he told you. (Mark 16:8)

The Ascension of Jesus
This same Jesus will come back. (Acts 1:11)

The Descent of the Holy Spirit at Pentecost
Each of us hears them preaching in our own language.
(Acts 2:8)

The Assumption of the Virgin Mary into Heaven
A great sign appeared in heaven. (Revelation 12:1)

The Coronation of Mary as Queen of Heaven and the
Glory of all the Saints
I saw a new heaven and a new earth. (Revelation 21:1)

More Information

For more information about Aylesford Priory, the prayer times of the Carmelite community, the pilgrimage calendar and facilities, and Carmelite vocations, please contact:

The Reception Office, The Friars, Aylesford, Kent, ME20 7BX, United Kingdom. Tel: +44 (0)1622 717272
E-mail: *reception@thefriars.org.uk*
Website of Aylesford Priory: *www.thefriars.org.uk*

For more information about the message of Carmel you might like to consult the following resources:

The British Province of Carmelites: *www.carmelite.org*

Carmelite Forum of Britain and Ireland: *www.carmeliteforum.org*

Carmelite Institute of Britain and Ireland: *www.cibi.ie*

International Carmelite Index: *www.carmelites.info*

John Welch, O.Carm., *The Carmelite Way: An Ancient Path for Today's Pilgrim*, (Leominster: Gracewing, 1996).

Wilfrid McGreal, O.Carm., *At the Fountain of Elijah: The Carmelite Tradition*, (London: Darton, Longman and Todd, 1999).

Joseph Chalmers, O.Carm. *The Sound of Silence: Listening to the Word of God with the prophet Elijah* (Faversham: Saint Albert's Press, 2007)

Emanuele Boaga, *The Lady of the Place: Mary in the History and in the Life of Carmel* (Rome: Edizioni Carmelitane, 2001)

Carmelite books are available from The Friars Bookshop, care of the address above.

Acknowledgements to Johan Bergström-Allen T.O.C and Fr Wilfrid McGreal, O.Carm. for their assistance while preparing the final text. For Johan Bergström-Allen T.O.C for the pictures.

Thérèse
Teacher of Prayer

St Thérèse of Lisieux has much to teach us about prayer. This delightfully simple booklet will help all who wish to follow the young Carmelite's way of praying with the heart.

The author, Brother Craig, takes us through some of the richest traditions: Eucharistic adoration, devotion to Our Lady and veneration of the saints and angels. Prayers to and by Thérèse are included.

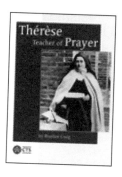

ISBN: 978 1 86082 480 7

CTS Code: D 693

Informative Catholic Reading

We hope that you have enjoyed reading this booklet.

If you would like to find out more about CTS booklets - we'll send you our free information pack and catalogue.

Please send us your details:

Name ....

Address ....

....

....

Postcode ....

Telephone...

Email ....

Send to: CTS, 40-46 Harleyford Road,
               Vauxhall, London
               SE11 5AY

Tel: 020 7640 0042
Fax: 020 7640 0046
Email: info@cts-online.org.uk